DEVELOPING THE ART OF DISCUSSION

DEVELOPING THE ART OF DISCUSSION

HANDBOOK FOR USE WITH CHURCH GROUPS

JOHN H. BUSHMAN/SANDY JONES

JUDSON PRESS ® VALLEY FORGE

DEVELOPING THE ART OF DISCUSSION

Copyright © 1977
Judson Press, Valley Forge, PA 19481

Library of Congress Cataloging in Publication Data

Bushman, John H.
  Developing the art of discussion.

  Bibliography: p. 57
  1. Discussion in Christian education—Handbooks, manuals, etc. I. Jones, Sandy, joint author.
II. Title.
BV1534.5.B87   268'.6   76-48524
ISBN 0-8170-0741-5

CONTENTS

THE NEED FOR DISCUSSION

The ability of individuals to communicate effectively with one another is one of the most important prerequisites for efficient community living. The interaction among individuals—sharing ideas, offering criticism, relating personal experiences, taking stands on issues—is absolutely necessary in order for the community to be alive, healthy, and productive. The community may be New York City, Kansas City, a senior English class, the Boys' Club, a Sunday evening youth group, and/or the middler class on Sunday morning. It is with these last two forms of community that we address ourselves for the remainder of this handbook. Effective communication can occur among individuals in the church school classroom if people take time to participate in discussion skills activities.

The church school classroom is a microcosm of the world around us. Patty, Jim, Connie, and Joe have been attending church together for some time. They realize each other's presence, but they really don't know each other. They are not aware of their feelings or what their thoughts are about current school, community, and church problems. Diane and Sam don't say very much in class primarily because of Ted. He giggles and snickers when his peers share their ideas. Then, of course, there is Judy. She talks and talks and talks; sometimes about the discussion topic, but most of the time about anything that happens to pop into her head. Steve and Karen are active, too. They have a common problem: not listening to the other's point of view. They argue a great deal; and while others present their views, Steve and Karen are busy preparing their rebuttals, not really hearing what their classmates have been saying.

We are sure that most, if not all, of these people appear in most church school classes. It is important for any church school teacher, then, to help students become aware of the need for effective classroom interaction and to provide them with the skills which will enable individuals to discuss openly and constructively. It is important for youngsters and adults, too, in church school to learn the process of a group—the process of how people talk together. Thus, discussion skills will help produce a cohesive group in which all students share responsibility for the proceedings of that group. Alfred Gorman, in his book *Teachers and Learners: The Interactive Process of Education,* suggests two reasons for working for group cohesiveness: (1) people tend to work toward their potential in a warm, supportive setting where they can concentrate on learning rather than on social needs and (2) the building of a cohesive group teaches people to be more self-directing, happier human beings.[1]

Another reason for the group process is that when people work effectively in this way, the exchange of ideas enhances learning, maturity, and self-direction. Group work enables individuals to draw from each other and participate in a process in which, as James Moffett suggests, "questioning, collaborating, qualifying, and calling for qualification, are habitual give-and-take operations."[2]

Many skill-building activities offer people a means to acquire effective group discussion techniques. These activities usually occur in the first few sessions of the church school class. In addition to using these activities at the beginning, teachers and/or group leaders may wish to incorporate them throughout the year as reinforcers. This reinforcing allows individuals to "practice" good group discussion techniques.

---

[1] Alfred Gorman, *Teachers and Learners: The Interactive Process of Education* (Boston: Allyn & Bacon, Inc., 1974), p. 33.
[2] James Moffett, *Drama: What Is Happening* (Champaign, Ill.: NCTE, 1967), p. 19.

Why discussion skills for the church school? It seems to us that church school members—children and adults—will benefit greatly from participating in a discussion skills program. Children will respond more freely and will feel more comfortable responding to their peers. Their ability and desire to interact will be greatly enhanced. Adults, too, enjoy the feeling that comes from reducing discussion inhibitions. They are able to respond more quickly and constructively. In addition, older children and adults see the need for participating in groups and extending the discussion so that the material presented in class can be thoroughly discussed.

We believe there are six important areas in which people can become competent with the skill-building activities, thus achieving competence in group discussion. The six areas should be included in a discussion skills program in the following sequence: getting acquainted, establishing trust, responsibility to participate, listening in discussion groups, roles in groups, and extending the discussion.

A SEQUENCE

GETTING ACQUAINTED

One of the most important considerations in the group process is for people to know one another. To know names is not enough; people must be aware of how each feels and what each thinks about current problems and issues. Knowing who each person is is one step in the process which enables individuals to feel more at ease when expressing themselves. If teachers want students to share their opinions, they must provide a classroom climate which is conducive to responses of this kind. Many assume that because students have been together in many classes over a period of time, they know each other. We warn against making such an assumption. Little more than names is usually known.

ESTABLISHING TRUST

A second vitally important step in helping people in the discussion process calls for them to trust one another. If Diane and Sam do not participate because of a fear of being laughed at or made fun of, the classroom is not conducive to effective group interaction. People can and must be tolerant of differing views as they are expressed in the classroom. Each has a right to express his/her opinion; but each has an obligation to listen carefully, to accept the idea for what it is, and to act in a courteous manner even though there may be disagreement.

Through a series of activities, students can have the opportunity to express themselves on various issues and can "practice" the structure which establishes a trustful rapport. Students will begin to share more and more of themselves as they begin to realize the supportive atmosphere around them. The trust activities will help develop confidence in the group process and in oneself, a sensitivity to others' wishes and feelings, and emotional control.

We are in no way recommending the use of sensitivity training or other similar processes. We feel strongly that these kinds of sessions in the hands of the unqualified are extremely dangerous. Trust activities should be very simple and nonthreatening. They help students to establish a strong, positive rapport with their peers; they are not intended as substitutes for counseling techniques and should not be used in that way.

RESPONSIBILITY TO PARTICIPATE

While it is a virtue to be a good listener, the group process cannot succeed if the group is comprised only of listeners! All participants have the responsibility to share their opinions and concerns in community interaction whether it be in a discussion of a Bible verse or in a discussion of the budget in a church business meeting. The job of getting everyone involved becomes easier after students have been through activities/games in getting acquainted and establishing trust; however, there still may be some who continually need a gentle nudge to participate. Students talk even more frequently once they see there is a definite *need* to interact. Activities described in this area help to provide that motivation needed for students to be aware of their responsibility to participate in the group interaction. One additional problem does exist. Some students may not participate because they can't; i.e., they have a problem getting into the discussion because a few other students dominate. The responsibility lies, then, in knowing when and how much to participate in group discussion. We recommend that teachers follow up the activities with an evaluation of the process. This can further indicate to students how the group process can work if everyone participates effectively.

12

LISTENING IN GROUPS

A severe problem in group discussion concerns individuals' unwillingness to listen carefully to each others' ideas. Too many times people share their ideas or positions and then plan their next responses while their peers are talking. When this happens, little progress is made. Often a select group of individuals argues over isolated points when in reality the participants are very close to an agreement, but they don't know it because they haven't listened to each other. Thus, activities must be planned to help people with their listening skills.

ROLES IN GROUPS

Individuals are not always cognizant of the many, varied roles that occur in discussion groups. Some are aware of the roles they are playing; some are not. Many teachers will recognize some, if not all, of the following character types that are played in their classes: silent member, discussion monopolizer, the clown, the yes-man, and the diplomat. If teachers provide experiences for students which emphasize these roles, a more effective discussion group may result as students adjust their behavior.

There are times when these activities may be used not only to highlight the existence of these roles but also to change specific behaviors of students. Teachers may use role playing and improvisations to put students in situations in which they perform roles with behavior that they normally do not exhibit.

EXTENDED DISCUSSION

Our experience suggests that students with the help of their teacher and these discussion skills activities develop a strong rapport conducive to effective interaction in group discussions. However, the problem with many of the discussions is that they fail to go beyond the surface level. Even after students know each other well and trust each other, they very seldom get to the core of the problem under discussion.

It is imperative that teachers provide students with experiences in which they have an opportunity to question, collaborate, and qualify, as Moffett suggests. Students need experiences in clarifying and justifying their statements; they need to have experiences in comparing and contrasting their positions with those of their peers; and, finally, they need to be placed in situations in which they can evaluate their own comments as well as those of the rest of the group. Through these processes students will move beyond the surface level and delve more deeply into the subject.

GROUP ORGANIZATION

Many times teachers wish to conduct their classroom in a total group setting. There are many objectives that are best achieved through an organization that would have the class act as one group. There are other times, however, when more effective teaching and learning can take place in small groups. Students often need opportunities to share their own thoughts and ideas. They need the give-and-take and support system of the small group. The practical method of providing students with enough language experiences and feedback lies in small group interaction. This arrangement allows a greater proportion of sharing time for each member and a more encouraging climate for members to experience.

How best to organize small groups is a concern of many teachers. Some feel it is important to select students for certain groups; others feel a random process can be just as effective. The following methods of grouping students for classroom activities may be appropriate:

1. Students are simply told to get into groups of a certain number (six or seven). The advantage is that students may be happier and more effective in the group if they have chosen that group. The disadvantage, of course, is this close

friendship may militate against productive work in the group. Also, some students may feel ostracized because they cannot get into a particular group.

2. Students are placed in groups at random. Each section of the class (four corners, center, etc.) makes a group. Little attention is given to having particular students in particular groups.

3. Students become members of groups by counting off. If six groups are desired, students number off up to six. Then all the 1s, 2s, and 3s, etc., get into groups.

It is well known that people spend much time in small groups. Human beings have needs that can only be satisfied with others. It is important that people be able to cooperate with each other when they are in these groups so that problems of living, working, and playing together can be solved. They must be able to solve these problems constructively. Skills in discussion provide tools for people to accomplish this task.

HOW TO USE THIS HANDBOOK

The activities in this handbook are grouped according to the areas just described. The amount of time spent in each area should be determined by the needs of the individual class. In a class with small children, activities in the first two areas may be sufficient and three to four weeks may be long enough. In a larger class of older children and adults, all activities in all areas may be appropriate and a longer time may be needed. Due to the nature of the church school class (the makeup of the class often changes from week to week), some of these activities should be repeated so that all students can receive full benefit.

Concentration on any one area of interaction alone may be desirable, and subject matter may be introduced at any time. It is important to remember, however, that relatively little open, meaningful discussion will take place until each class member feels comfortable in contributing. Once the class has moved on to another phase of the program, there may be a need for reinforcement of particular skills; therefore, some of these activities may be used as reinforcers whenever this need appears. These activities are indicated by #.

We strongly recommend that each activity be followed by a

general discussion. It is imperative that the teacher discuss the results of the activity in terms of its objectives. The following questions might be helpful in discussing the activities:

GETTING ACQUAINTED

1. How has the activity changed the atmosphere of the class?
2. Do the students feel more at ease with one another?
3. In what ways did students interact verbally and nonverbally?
4. Has the activity facilitated the learning of names?
5. Are students aware of the individual personalities of members of the group?

ESTABLISHING TRUST

1. How has this activity strengthened trust among members of the group?
2. To what degree, if any, did members feel threatened by the activity?
3. How has the establishment of trust strengthened the cohesiveness of the group?
4. Has the activity facilitated the learning of the class? If so, in what ways?
5. Do you feel comfortable now to share ideas and feelings that you feel strongly about?

RESPONSIBILITY TO PARTICIPATE

1. Did each student accept the responsibility to participate? If not, discuss why.
2. Do students feel the need to participate because their ideas have value or because it is required by the activity?

LISTENING IN GROUPS

1. How did students feel about the limitations imposed by the structure of the activity?
2. When would this structure be beneficial to effective group interaction?
3. What factors inhibit good listening?
4. How has this activity made students aware of their individual needs for listening skill building as well as the need for listening in groups?

**ROLES
IN
GROUPS**

1. What roles evolved during the course of this activity?
2. To what extent is it important for roles to be established in groups?
3. How has this activity helped students to identify roles they play in group discussion?
4. What are the advantages and disadvantages of discussion groups which are composed of a variety of roles or just one role?

**EXTENDED
DISCUSSION**

1. How does extending the levels of discussion create more meaningful interaction?
2. How has this activity enabled students to examine the discussion topic more thoroughly and/or to achieve a clearer understanding of the problem?

At the risk of overstructuring the use of these activities, we have recommended an age group for each of the activities. For convenience, we have used the following symbols next to the title of the activity to designate the age group: P (ages 5-8); I (ages 9-12); YA (ages 13-18); A (adults); and AA (all ages).

ACTIVITIES

GETTING ACQUAINTED

For students to feel comfortable contributing in groups, they must first know the people with whom they will be interacting. The activities in this area are aimed at simply "breaking the ice," getting individuals to meet and learn something about each other. These activities must precede all others since success in the other areas is dependent on satisfactory completion of this phase.

Early activities involve only the learning of names by association. Toward the end of this phase, individuals should know not only names of people but also enough about them so that they become personalities as well as familiar faces. People are asked to interact with their peers, thereby breaking down inhibitive barriers, which is an important step toward acceptance and the next phase—establishing trust.

Discussion of Scripture, Bible stories, and personal values demands a familiar and comfortable relationship among individuals in the group. It is important to emphasize the need for continual use of these getting-acquainted activities as new people join the class.

TWENTY-FIVE QUESTIONS (I, YA, A)

Activity: Distribute copies of Twenty-five Questions to students.
Instruct participants to secure signatures from individuals

who meet the requirements listed on the handout. No more than two signatures should be obtained from any one person. Individuals should not volunteer information but simply respond to questions.

Possible questions:

A person whose family owns a Volkswagen

A person who has at least five pennies in his/her pocket

A person who lives in a split-level house

A person who lives on a dead-end street

A person who has lived in a foreign country

A person who likes licorice

A person who can recite the first four books of the New Testament

A person who is wearing brown pants

A person who has all four grandparents living

A person who has been on television

A person who has a cocker spaniel

A person who has four brothers and/or sisters

A person who is a member of a Scout troop

A person who has a Snoopy bath towel

A person who likes liver

A person who has sung in a church choir

A person who has the same number of letters in his/her name as you do

A person who vacations out of the state

A person who speaks a language other than English

A person who can recite a Bible passage

A person who competes in swimming

A person who wants to teach in a college/university

A person who has been in a church play

A person who has had his/her appendix removed

A person who can recite the Twenty-third Psalm

I.D. TAGS (AA)

Activity: Pin a name or place tag to the back of each student. Instruct students to seek their identities by asking each classmate no more than three questions which can be answered with a "yes" or "no." While this is not a contest to see who is first or last, students may wish to sit down after learning their identities to observe the remaining portion of this activity. Tags could include biblical and/or contemporary names and places.

Possible Biblical Names or Places:		Possible Contemporary Names or Places:	
Paul	Adam	Charlie Brown	Chris Evert
Jesus	Eve	Mickey Mouse	Walt Disney
Jerusalem	Mary	Batman	Lassie
Matthew	Joseph	Grand Canyon	Martin Luther King, Jr.
Mark	Bethlehem	Washington, D.C.	John Kennedy
Luke	Nazareth	Billy Graham	Mary Tyler Moore
John	Mount Sinai	George Washington	Johnny Carson
Peter	Judas	Evel Knievel	Uncle Sam
Galilee	Pontius Pilate	Babe Ruth	Helen Keller
Moses	John the Baptist	Billy Jean King	John Wayne

OCCUPATION GEMS (YA, A)

Activity: Distribute slips of paper with names of "occupations" to one-half of the class and names of "stones" to the other half. Instruct students to find the person who has the best match for their "stone" or "occupation." The matched pair may then be seated. When all are seated, answers may be checked by having students state their names, their stones, and their correct occupations.

OCCUPATION GEMS ANSWER KEY

1. Surgeon	Bloodstone	10. Demanding boss	Grindstone
2. German fisherman	Rhinestone	11. Shoemaker	Cobblestone
3. Citrus grower	Limestone	12. Color guard	Flagstone
4. Undertaker	Tombstone	13. Coward	Yellowstone
5. Dairyman	Milk stone	14. Prospector	Gold stone
6. Politician	Blarney stone	15. Landlord	Brownstone
7. Architect	Cornerstone	16. Tire salesman	Firestone
8. Locksmith	Keystone	17. Daredevil	Gall stone
9. Motorist	Milestone	18. Indian chief	Flintstone

BACKPACKING # (AA)

Activity: Seat students in a circle. Have students fit their names and an item which begins with the same initial sound as their first name in an introduction: "I'm Tom; I'm going backpacking; and I'm going to bring a tent." Susan, the next student in the circle, introduces herself in a similar way: "My name is Susan and I'm going on a backpacking trip with Tom. I'm going to take a sleeping bag." The process continues around the circle with each student introducing himself/herself and renaming all those students who have preceded. Halfway around the circle, have those students who have given their names change places with each other, so the order of this list of names changes; and, therefore, the emphasis is placed on names and faces rather than a memory of a sequence.

ALLITERATION # (AA)

Activity: (part one) Seat students in a circle. Instruct students to think of an adjective that alliterates with their first names. Going around the circle, students say their adjective and first names, for example, Jumping Jack, Silly Sandy. After completing the circle, have students attempt to name as many in the circle as possible. During this process, have students who are yet to be named switch places. Another variation which can be used as a follow-up activity is to have one student repeat his/her adjective and name and call on another person in the circle by adjective and name. Have the student whose name has just been called repeat his/her alliteration and call out someone else's alliteration until everyone in the circle has been named.

(part two) With students still in a circle, have them add an alliterative verb to their adjective and name and complete the circle a second time, for example, Jumping Jack Jogs, Silly Sandy Sits. Use the same follow-up procedure as stated in part one.

CATEGORIES OF THREE (AA)

Activity: Instruct students to share three things they enjoy doing ending in "ing." Continue this activity until everyone has contributed and has become better acquainted.

PERSONAL INVENTORIES (I, YA, A)[1]

Activity: Have students draw a box in the center of a sheet of paper. In the box they must write their name and list three things they do well. Then they are to draw lines from the corner points of the box to the corner edges of the paper, forming four sections. In the top section they list three books they have recently read (three movies seen, three TV programs they enjoy, etc.); in the left section, they list three things they want to learn to do; in the bottom section, they list three things they hate to do, but must do; in the right section, they list three things they do poorly. Display papers around the room for sharing.

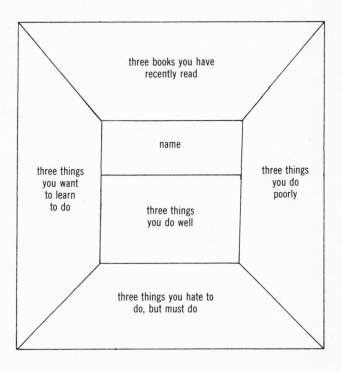

[1] The authors are indebted to Dr. Rich Hause, Professor of Curriculum and Instruction, Kansas State University, for the idea of this activity.

25

LONDON BRIDGE # (P)

Activity: Place children in a circle. Select two to form the bridge. Play the game London Bridge with the following song:

"London Bridge is falling down, falling down, falling down.

London Bridge is falling down, my fair (child's name).

Tell us something you can do, you can do, you can do.

Tell us something you can do, my fair (child's name)."

At this point, the child in the bridge states something he/she can do. The child is then released to sit down and the circle continues. When everyone has been in the bridge, the group sings the verses to the bridge makers and they respond.

Other verses:

"Tell us something you'd like to be."

"Tell us somewhere you'd like to go."

"Tell us something you'd like to do."

"Tell us someone you'd like to be."

NAMING A CHARACTER . . . (I, YA, A)

Activity: Have students consider a character, an idea, or a concept in the Bible, other literature, a film, or in real life that they admire. Have students share these by either contributing around the circle or responding. As a second activity, have students share a dislike.

Variation for P age group:
Have children name a person in a Bible story that they like and tell why.

INTERVIEW CARDS (I, YA, A)

Activity: Divide the class into pairs. Make a set of Interview Cards for each pair. Instruct them to select one card at a time and ask the information of each other. Students will use the information they have gathered when they introduce each other to the rest of the class. They may use the cards for easy reference when making the introductions. Possible questions for cards include:

26

If you were a president now, what would be your first directive?

What is the most pressing problem America is facing today?

What do you like most about this church?

If you could pick your own name, what name would you choose?

On a rainy day would you rather listen to music, read, sleep, or walk in the rain?

What is your favorite season of the year?

What is your favorite Bible story and why?

Name a place you'd like to visit.

What do you consider to be your major strength?

What do you consider to be your major weakness?

What would you change in this church school class?

Variation for P age group:

Follow the above procedure substituting the cards on the next page. Have each child choose his/her favorite from each card and tell why.

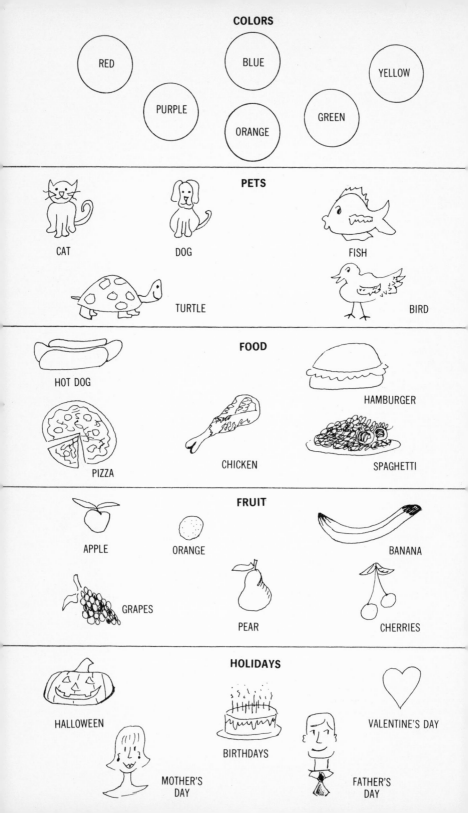

COLORS

RED

BLUE

PURPLE

YELLOW

ORANGE

GREEN

PETS

CAT

DOG

FISH

TURTLE

BIRD

FOOD

HOT DOG

HAMBURGER

PIZZA

CHICKEN

SPAGHETTI

FRUIT

APPLE

ORANGE

BANANA

GRAPES

PEAR

CHERRIES

HOLIDAYS

HALLOWEEN

VALENTINE'S DAY

BIRTHDAYS

MOTHER'S DAY

FATHER'S DAY

NAME SHOOTING # (AA)

Activity: Have students clear a space in the classroom where they may move around freely. With all students standing in a group, instruct them to move about the room. Whenever a student meets the glance of another person, he/she must "draw" or point to that person and say that person's first name before the other can say his/hers. The winner of the "shoot-out" continues mingling, while the other person sits down. Eventually there should be two left who will "duel," and the winner is the person who has most successfully and quickly named everyone he/she has met.

NAME QUIZ # (AA)

Activity: Prepare a quiz consisting of questions based on information that students in the class have revealed about themselves through interaction and interviews; for example, "Who has the desire to live in Fairbanks, Alaska?" The answer is the name of the person who shared this desire with the class.

ESTABLISHING TRUST

This area is probably the most important for basic interaction. Although students may now associate names with faces and personalities, they may still not know how they are accepted by these people. The volunteer activity is an excellent way to diagnose the lack of acceptance and trust in the class. Students must realize that their frustration and reluctance in interacting is shared by all and is not a problem unique to them. The following activities help students not only to discover their own lack of trust but also to develop trust among members of the class so that free and honest interaction can occur without fear of rejection.

The early activities are fairly nonthreatening, since they involve mostly written responses and oral responses by choice. The later activities are a little more demanding. They ask the students to commit themselves to an issue of controversy. Other activities require students to explore themselves and to help the class understand each other by sharing ideas and feelings.

A word of caution needs to be expressed here since some of these activities could touch upon very personal experiences in a student's

30

life. No one should be forced to respond. Individuals should be asked to share only those ideas and feelings which they can comfortably discuss in public.

Time spent in this area should also be determined by the needs of the group. This area is so vital to successful interaction, however, that a class should not proceed to the next phase until everyone feels accepted. If at a later time someone seems uncomfortable, it may be desirable to return to some of these activities to rebuild any trust that seems to have been lost.

Due to the nature of the discussion which occurs in many church school classes, trust is essential. Individuals not only will interpret Scripture and Bible stories but also will be confronted with varying value systems which they should compare, contrast, and evaluate. For example, after reading the parable of the good Samaritan, the class may want to go beyond the obvious question—Who is my neighbor? Questions which require a more personal response include: Are you sometimes like the priest and/or the Levite? Why do you think people in today's society are reluctant to get involved? Have you ever had a problem that no one was willing to help you solve? Is it more difficult to help those whom you know do not like you? What are some of the considerations that you would make before becoming "a good Samaritan"?

VOLUNTEERS (I, YA, A)

Activity: Without further explanation, ask for three to five volunteers to come to the front of the room. Do not answer any questions or elaborate in any way. Wait as long as it takes to get the number of volunteers for which you asked. After the students have come forward, tell them they may be seated, explaining that there is nothing for them to do. Follow this with a discussion of why those people decided to volunteer, why the others did not, and what went through their minds during the wait.

While this activity involves trust primarily, it may also be used prior to getting acquainted activities as an introduction to the need for the entire discussion skills program.

"WHO AM I?" (I, YA, A)

Activity: Have students write "I am..." on a sheet of paper, followed by five items that would accurately complete the statement as it applies to them at that moment.

> Sample: I am talkative.
> excited about this church school class.
> worried about the game Friday night.
> concerned about Susan's health.
> pleased with my family relationship.

Students may voluntarily share these statements with the class or respond after being called upon by another student.

Variation for P group:
My name is _____.
I look something like this.

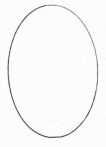

Here is something that makes me happy.

Here is something that makes me sad.

By sharing this information about themselves, students begin to learn more personal items about each other and thus develop a stronger bond in the group.

"I LIKE PEOPLE WHO . . ." (AA)

Activity: Instruct students to complete on paper or orally partial statements that you read to them. The following are statements that you may wish to include in your list:

> I like people who . . .
> In my spare time I love to . . .
> The best thing about school is . . .
> It makes me mad when . . .
> I wish my parents/children wouldn't . . .
> I feel best when I'm with a group of people who . . .
> I feel worst when I'm with a group of people who . . .
> When I'm around adults/small children, I feel . . .
> Strangers make me feel . . .
> When I'm 20/30/60/80, I think I'll be . . .
> When there is no "right answer," I feel . . .
> Other people regard me as . . .

Discuss the responses to each of these on a voluntary basis. If students seem reluctant to discuss the last statement—"Other people regard me as . . ."—discuss why this is true. These statements reveal personal feelings, goals, and anxieties which can only be shared honestly as trust develops in a group.

FACES (AA)

Activity: Have students draw their expressions on the following faces in reaction to the statements below. By sharing their drawings they are revealing aspects of their personalities, an important step in the development of trust in the group.

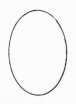
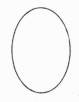

1. An expensive baby-sitter is coming.

2. Our dog is lost.

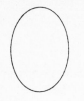

3. I have opened a present I love.

4. I must go to another committee meeting.

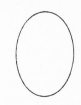

5. We are having cauliflower for dinner.

6. I haven't completed my speech.

FEELINGS AND WISHES (AA)

Activity: Complete the following in the space provided:
This is how I feel today:

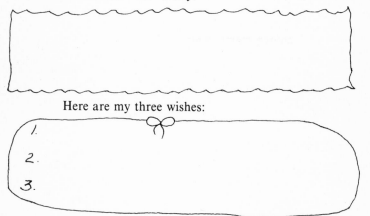

Here are my three wishes:

1.

2.

3.

Individuals may volunteer to share their responses with the class. Sharing these feelings and wishes will bring the group closer together.

VALUE CONTINUUM # (I, YA, A)

Activity: Distribute copies of a Value Continuum to students. Instruct them to mark the appropriate place on the continuum indicating their response to statements that you read to them. "A" represents "strongly agree"; "Z" represents "strongly disagree." Statements that you choose should be slightly controversial and of interest to students. The following is a list of possible statements:

People would be happier if everyone went to church.

The movie rating system should be informative, but not restrictive.

The government should use money to clean up rivers and pollution before feeding indigent families.

If a person is starving, it is justifiable for that person to steal.

Young people run away from home to prove their maturity.

Sustaining life by artificial means is against God's will.

War can be fought in the name of God.

The most important thing Jesus taught was forgiveness.

Someone is not a Christian unless he/she is a member of a church.

A person's life-style should not prohibit him/her from church membership.

Students' responses in this activity as well as in the next activity, Value Voting, test the degree to which trust has been established. In addition, these statements require participants to commit themselves to a position which in itself helps to establish trust.

VALUE VOTING # (I, YA, A)

Activity: Instruct students to respond in the following manner to a list of statements you give them:

raised arm, hand waving	strongly agree
raised arm	agree
arms folded across chest	choose not to respond
hands folded	indifferent
arm extended, thumb down	disagree
arm extended, thumb down, stirring	strongly disagree

35

The statements should be controversial and of interest to students. The following is a list of possible statements:

The age at which persons may buy beer should be lowered to sixteen.

People should be allowed to drive at age fourteen with no restrictions.

There should be a smoking lounge for students established in high schools.

Capital punishment is a valid, reasonable form of crime control.

Hunger and starvation exist because people will not help themselves.

A law should be passed restricting the number of children per family.

Church school classes should be intergenerational rather than age-restrictive.

Memorization of Bible verses should be an integral part of church school.

SHADOW PORTRAIT (AA)

Activity: Working with a partner, have individuals outline each other lying on a large sheet of paper (butcher or newsprint). After cutting out the figures, students should fill in the designated areas in the following manner:

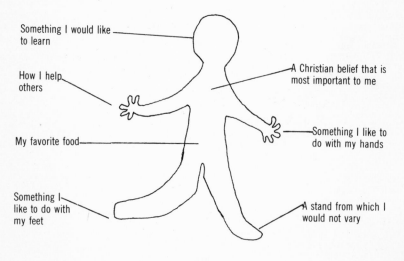

Something I would like to learn

How I help others

My favorite food

Something I like to do with my feet

A Christian belief that is most important to me

Something I like to do with my hands

A stand from which I would not vary

36

When finished, share the portraits. An atmosphere of deeper trust evolves from the sharing of values expressed through the portraits.

COAT OF ARMS (I, YA, A)

Activity: Using the following coat of arms, have all persons complete the sections by drawing and/or writing their responses to the following statements:
  1. The thing that makes you most angry.
  2. The goal you most want to achieve.
  3. The one gift you would give the world.
  4. Something you are good at/something you would like to be good at.
  5. A value from which you would never deviate.
  6. A word you would like others to use to describe you.
  7. A color that represents you.
  8. A value by which your family lives.

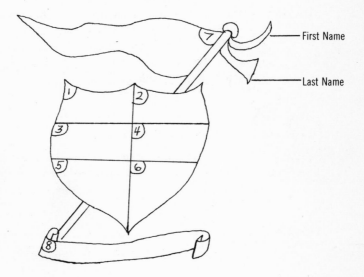

Share and display.

SAFE-DEPOSIT BOX (I, YA, A)

Activity: Using shoe boxes or similar containers, create three safe-deposit boxes labeled "Treasures," "Hopes," and "Fears." Have students write three things in their lives that make them the most happy and why these things make them happy. After sharing, have students write their names on the paper and then place their treasures in the Treasure Box. Repeat this procedure for their hopes and fears.

Hopes: Three things you want most to happen in your life.

Fears: Three fears you have for yourself, your family, and/or the world.

At some future date, the class may wish to look at their "deposits" and reevaluate their treasures, hopes, and fears.

"ME BAGS" (I, YA, A)[2]

Activity: Distribute paper bags to each student. Place magazines, crayons, glue, and scissors in a convenient location. Instruct students to think of the paper bags as themselves. On the outside they must glue pictures, headlines, phrases, or words cut from the magazines which they feel describe how others see them. On the inside, students should indicate how they see themselves. If material is not readily available, students may draw on the bags. It may be desirable to require a maximum of three symbols per side. Students share their bags and explain some or all of their symbols.

IN-DEPTH INTERVIEW (I, YA, A)

Activity: Place students in pairs or small groups. Instruct students to interview each other once again, asking questions which will help them to understand the other person's point of view on various ideas.

GROUP COOPERATION (I, YA, A)

Activity: Have the class respond to the following question: "What

---

[2] The authors are indebted to Debby Connor, graduate student, School of Education, University of Kansas, for the idea for this activity.

can each of us do to make each other feel comfortable and free to respond in discussion?"

ANIMAL, VEGETABLE, CITY (I, YA, A)

Activity: Have each student name an animal, a vegetable or fruit, and a city that is most like him/her and tell why.

Example: cocker spaniel—somewhat dependent, affectionate

onion—multilayered, enhances other things

New Orleans—the past as well as the future is important

This activity, as well as the next three, asks participants to share their own self-concepts, which would be difficult without the establishment of trust.

SYMBOL SHARING (AA)

Activity: Using paper and crayons, each student is to create a symbol which represents him/her. Share symbols with class and discuss their meanings.

AUTOBIOGRAPHICAL PICTURES (I, YA, A)

Activity: Arrange class in a circle. Instruct students to write a simple autobiography on paper using only symbols or pictures, no words. It must be organized and clear enough that someone else can read it and learn something about that student. When students are finished, have them sign their names and exchange papers with someone else. Have student "read" his/her partner's autobiography, showing the symbols used. The author should be given some time to respond to the interpretation of his/her story.

CHILDREN'S STORIES (AA)

Activity: Instruct students to consider an experience in their lives unique to them. From children's books which you or the class members have provided, have students select a character (animal or human) with which they identify in this experience. Students should relate the experience, showing those pictures in the book which illustrate it.

CHILDHOOD TABLE (I, YA, A)

Activity: On a sheet of paper, have students draw with colored pencils or crayons an overhead view of the dinner table of their childhood. Students are to create a symbol and choose a particular color which represents each member of the family as they sat around the table. Share these drawings and discuss the meaning of the symbols and colors.

RESPONSIBILITY TO PARTICIPATE

This third phase of developing discussion skills concentrates on the need for everyone in a group to participate. At this point students should know each other and feel comfortable interacting but may either dominate discussions or feel no need to contribute. The following activities are structured to demonstrate to students the necessity for their contribution in discussion and to force them to accept the responsibility of being contributing members of their group.

At this point in the sequence, if students are not participating in discussions, it is not because they do not know and trust members of the group, but because they do not feel their contribution is valuable or their opportunity to contribute is limited by those dominating discussions.

The first activity is an artificial discussion with an emphasis on the process of the interaction rather than on the solution of a problem. Students may feel frustrated with the restriction or resentful at being forced to contribute; yet the focus is on just those problems. The class should discuss the value of equal contribution in groups. Much later the class may need to return to this activity to discipline themselves in discussion.

The Neidt Game points to the necessity for everyone's participation. It also gets students out of their seats and into physical, as well as verbal, interaction. As an observer, the teacher may use this and the following activity as a diagnostic tool to evaluate the group process.

In the Crossword Puzzle activity, students begin with a tangible contribution to make when they move into the groups. Therefore, everyone has something to contribute if he/she so chooses. The importance of contributing becomes evident when a team could have improved its score by one or two points if students had only seen "Johnny's" puzzle. At this point, it is good to show that not only does each student have the responsibility to contribute in a group, but also the group has a responsibility to seek out that contribution.

CONTRIBUTIONS (I, YA, A)

Activity: Divide the class into groups of five to seven each and select a topic for discussion. During the discussion each student must contribute at least once and at random. No student can participate twice until all have participated once.

THE NEIDT GAME # (YA, A)[3]

Activity: Using the model below, create ten game cards and randomly distribute them. If class size is less than ten, some people will need to receive two cards in sequence. Students are to form the well-known saying "We are one in the Spirit" by positioning themselves in a circle. The front side of the colored card contains portions of words in the saying; the reverse side contains additional clues as to its position in the circle. The model cards are numbered for the instructor's convenience; however, student cards should not be numbered.

MODEL: (Front Side)

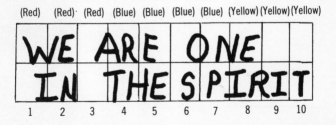

---

[3] The authors are indebted to Kyle and Bill Neidt, graduate students, School of Education, University of Kansas, for the idea of this activity.

(Back Side)

1. Red likes Red.
   Red likes Yellow.
   Red faces Blue.
2. Red likes Red.
   Red faces Blue.
3. Red likes Blue.
   Red likes Red.
   Red faces Blue.
4. Blue likes Blue.
   Blue likes Red.
   Blue faces Yellow.
5. Blue likes Blue.
   Blue faces Yellow.

6. Blue likes Blue.
   Blue faces Red.
7. Blue likes Blue.
   Blue likes Yellow.
   Blue faces Red.
8. Yellow likes Blue.
   Yellow likes Yellow.
   Yellow faces Red.
9. Yellow likes Yellow.
   Yellow faces Blue.
10. Yellow likes Yellow.
    Yellow likes Red.
    Yellow faces Blue.

CROSSWORD PUZZLES # (YA, A)[4]

Activity: Distribute copies of the crossword puzzles to each student. Instruct students to fill in the puzzles using as many different letters as possible to form words. Abbreviations, foreign or obsolete words, and words beginning with a

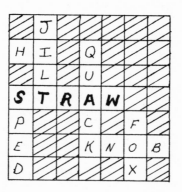

[4] The authors are indebted to Sharon Murphy, Jefferson West High, Meriden, Kansas, for the idea of this activity. The puzzle was created by Martha Bushman, Ottawa, Kansas.

capital letter are not allowed. Score one point for *each different letter* used for the individual score. Distributed puzzles include word "straw" only.

Divide class into groups of five to seven each. Have students compare individual puzzles working as a team to complete one puzzle. Score the group puzzle the same as for the individual puzzles to arrive at a team grand total. Compare these scores with other teams. Perfect score is twenty-one points.

SYMBOL GROUPING # (AA)

Activity: Make symbol cards (see below) out of different colored paper. Distribute these cards to participants, instructing them to organize themselves in groups according to the symbols. To do this, individuals will need to find the characteristic which is common to the others in the group.

Note: The common characteristic should *not* be the color of the card.

For example, in a class of twelve, each student would receive a symbol from one of the groups. Increase the number of symbols in any one group to accommodate any change in class number by creating either a copy of an existing symbol or a new one with a similar characteristic.

Symbols:

Key: There are three groups.

    Group 1—curved lines

    Group 2—straight lines

    Group 3—combination of curved and straight lines

        This activity requires students to contribute information to solve a problem. From this structured interaction students will demonstrate the need for participation in groups.

LISTENING IN GROUPS

The activities in this area are designed to accomplish two things: to demonstrate the need for skills in listening and to develop these skills in groups. Although students understand the responsibility to contribute, they may be overzealous, concentrating so much on their participation that they do not listen to what others say. The typical situation arising from a heated discussion, wherein two students are arguing over a point on which they agree, can be eliminated if students further discipline themselves to listen. These activities may frustrate students since they are rigidly structured to force students to listen when they may wish very much to contribute; therefore, each activity must be followed by discussion of student response, value of the activity, and fulfillment of purpose.

SUMMARY-AGREEMENT-OPINION # (AA)

Activity: Divide class into groups of five to seven and select a topic for discussion. The topic should be slightly controversial to provide differing opinions. During the discussion each student must follow this pattern: (1) summarize the preceding person's statement, (2) state points with which he/she agrees, and (3) give his/her own opinion.

STORY BUILDING (AA)

Activity: Place students in a circle. Have one student begin a story. The story develops as each student repeats the story and adds to it. This activity encourages creativity and is dependent upon listening for a unified story line. The teacher may wish to have the student who began the story relate the whole story from beginning to end.

INTERACTION CARDS # (I, YA, A)

Activity: Using the models provided, create sets of Interaction Cards. Place students in groups of six. If class size prohibits equal distribution in groups of six, place remaining students as follows: if three or less, place one in each of the existing groups, having each student use an extra Interaction Card (in groups of seven, two students will be using cards with the same color and will need to alternate their use); if four or more, place in a new group having some students use more than one Interaction Card. *An important note:* the color code is used to indicate sequence of interaction only; students should be referred to by name, not by color.

Each group should use the six cards. The sequence of interaction is Blue, Red, Green, Yellow, Orange, Purple. Cards should be distributed at random to eliminate the "going-around-the-circle" technique.

Give students the topic for discussion. A single topic may be used by all groups, or each group may have its own. In either case, the topic should be of current interest. The interaction sequence may now begin.

If a question is directed to a student out of sequence, that student should respond. Students should then return to the sequence.

The interaction can be stopped at any time; however, for best results, students should complete three rounds.

After completing the three rounds, students should discuss the activity. Were they able to follow the directions on the Interaction Cards? Why? Why not? In what ways was listening difficult? What is needed to participate effectively? What are some examples of communication breakdown due to lack of listening? How important is the interaction among peers in the classroom? In church school? In the community? The class should discuss group interaction, its techniques, and its importance.

A SAMPLE ROUND

Topic: Churches should take stands on political issues.

1. Mary (Blue) gives her opinion on the topic: "I believe the

Interaction Cards

GREEN

1. Ask question of Red or Blue.

2. Respond to Red.

3. Point out differences between Purple's idea and others previously made.

PURPLE

1. Show relationship between Orange's and Blue's ideas.

2. Introduce new idea—your opinion.

3. Summarize position of group at this point.

RED

1. Agree or disagree with previous statement (Blue's) and tell why.

2. Justify Orange's and/or Blue's idea.

3. Respond to Blue's idea.

ORANGE

1. Introduce new idea—your opinion.

2. Summarize position of group at this point.

3. Ask question of either Yellow or Green.

BLUE

1. Give your opinion on topic.

2. Clarify your position.

3. Give example of previous idea (Purple's).

YELLOW

1. Respond to Red's or Blue's answer.

2. Expand upon Red's, Blue's, or Green's response.

3. Point out similarities between Purple's idea and others previously made.

church has a responsibility to take political stands because historically the Christian church has been instrumental in changing society for the better."

2. Bob (Red) agrees or disagrees with Mary's (Blue) statement and tells why: "I disagree. I don't think the church could arrive at a stand that represents every member's point of view."

3. Jennifer (Green) ask Bob (Red) or Mary (Blue) a question: "If the church would represent the majority's stand on an issue, isn't that the democratic way that most church business is run?"

4. Bob (Red) answers: "Yes, I guess so."

5. Cliff (Yellow) responds to Bob (Red) or Mary (Blue): "I agree with Mary. The early churches certainly had an effect on the society of the time. Paul's contribution also affected the Roman power structure."

6. Amy (Orange) introduces a new idea: "I see a danger in the church becoming politically active. What if people joined churches just because of their political views, like joining a political party?"

7. Chip (Purple) shows relationship between Amy's (Orange) and Mary's (Blue) ideas: "Even though Amy and Mary disagree on taking a political stand, they both imply that the church has powerful influence in the community."

ROLES IN GROUPS

Students have probably been aware of the emergence of a leadership role in their groups, but it is also important to investigate the other roles that exist and to show their interchangeability. Each of the activities in this group, except Role-Playing Cards, allows the roles to emerge spontaneously without direction. These activities are good for evaluating the roles and observing the exchange of roles.

The Role-Playing Cards force a student to play a specific role to examine the behavior typical of that role. The teacher may wish to use the Role-Playing Cards to try to change the behavior of participants by giving selected roles to students who exhibit opposite behavior; for example, giving the Dominator-Monopolizer role to a student who does not participate frequently.

CALCULATION # (I, YA, A)

Activity: Divide class into groups of five to seven each. Have each group calculate the average number of brothers and sisters of the members of the group. The first to finish should stand up. Discuss how leadership evolved in the group.

ALPHABETIZING # (AA)

Activity: Place individual letters of the alphabet on cards from A to the letter which corresponds to the number of people in the group. Give everyone an alphabet card. When all cards have been distributed, tell students to "alphabetize" themselves in a single line or large circle. Watch for specific roles as they develop in this activity. Discuss if and how leadership roles changed.

MYSTERY GAME # (YA, A)

Activity: Distribute the clues listed below to members of the class. Some may get more than one clue, depending on the size of the class. Tell them to look at their clues and to begin the activity after you read the following directions: "An apparent kidnapping has been committed. Using your clues, you, as a group, must discover who committed the crime. Clues may only be exchanged verbally, and no more than three of you may be out of your seat at any one time. Your decision must be reached through consensus. If any part of your decision is incorrect or incomplete, I will tell you it is wrong."

The following clues should be used in this mystery game:

1. Mrs. Richblood discovered a letter on her daughter's desk that night.
2. Miss Sugar told investigators that Theodore True was always complaining about the financial burden of dating Rosiland Richblood.
3. The head of the campus women's liberation movement, Ms. Libby Free, told police that Rosiland Richblood did not want to marry.
4. Carl "Robin" Hood, long-haired veteran and leader of

the radical campus group R. O. R. (Rip Off the Rich), was seen with Rosiland Richblood at the Student Union Grill at 4:00 P.M.

5. Theodore True told Richard Richblood, Jr., Carl Hood was a drug addict.
6. Mr. Richblood told authorities Theodore had tried to see Rosiland at 10:45 P.M. but was refused admittance.
7. Mrs. Richblood said Richard, Jr., had gone to a meeting on campus at 8:00 P.M.
8. The voice on the telephone was that of a man.
9. The letter revealed that Rosiland and Theodore had had a serious argument.
10. Richard Richblood, Jr., told authorities Theodore True wanted to marry his sister for her money.
11. Theodore True had proposed to Rosiland Richblood.
12. Carl Hood told newsmen the wealth in the country needed to be equally distributed for economic survival.
13. Mr. Richard Richblood was not in favor of a marriage between his daughter and True.
14. Rosiland Richblood left her home at 7:15 P.M. for the library.
15. The Richbloods received a call at 12:05 A.M. asking for $50,000 for the return of their daughter, Rosiland.
16. Libby Free told authorities that Richblood, Jr., had not shown up for his meeting.
17. Carl Hood was picked up for hitchhiking by a state highway patrolman at 11:45 P.M. and arrested for possession of marijuana.
18. Dr. Boris Daly, professor of political science, said Hood was an interested student, but that he seemed radical in his hatred of the wealthy.
19. Buddy Pal, a local used car dealer, reportedly sold a green and white '57 Chevy to a young man wearing an old army jacket. The man paid for the car in cash at 10:15 P.M.
20. Mr. Richard E. Richblood was a trustee of Slick Stone College in Maple, New Hampshire.
21. Nadine Sugar works at the Student Union Grill from 3:00 to 11:00 P.M.

22. It takes twenty minutes to get from the Richblood home to the library.
23. Richblood said his son had become a "free spirit" and understanding was lost between them.
24. Mrs. Richblood said her daughter's values had changed drastically in the past few months.
25. Miss Sugar revealed that Miss Richblood had met Hood in the Grill and had been seen with him occasionally.
26. Nadine (Bunny) Sugar reported she had seen Rosiland Richblood give money to Carl Hood.
27. A neighbor saw a young man wearing an old army jacket force Miss Richblood into a 1957 Chevy at approximately 11:50 P.M.
28. Ms. Free told reporters that Miss Richblood had been unhappy at home.
29. Theodore True met Nadine Sugar at the Student Union as she was getting off work. They went to a movie.
30. Dr. Daly saw Rosiland leave the library at 10:30 P.M.
31. Richard Richblood, Jr., served in the armed forces.
32. Ms. Free revealed that Richblood, Jr., was very protective of his sister.
33. The name of Rosiland Richblood was found on the membership roll of the R. O. R.
34. The Richbloods received a call from their son at 10:00 P.M. with the message that he would be staying with a friend from the college that night.
35. Ms. Free reported that Rosiland worshiped her brother.

Solution: Richard and Rosiland Richblood conspired in an extortion of their parents.

ROLE-PLAYING CARDS # (I, YA, A)

Activity: Create Role-Playing Cards using roles listed below. Divide the class into groups of eight. (Teachers may wish to use only a portion of the class for this activity. If so, students not role-playing may observe their peers and guess specific roles that are performed.) Distribute the Role-Playing Cards to students at random; give the group a topic to discuss; and tell the students to discuss the subject from the point of view and in the manner of the role suggested on the cards.

Roles for cards:

Diplomat	Hostile Agressor
Yes-Man	Dominator/Monopolizer
Silent Member	Humanitarian
Clown	Logical Reasoner

Discuss the activity following the role playing. Have the class point out advantages and disadvantages when church school discussion groups are made up of students with a variety of these traits or with just one of these traits.

EXTENDED DISCUSSION CARDS # (YA, A)

Many discussion groups develop a rapport conducive to much group interaction but often fail to discuss topics in any depth. The Extended Discussion Cards enable students to probe, a process in which students are encouraged to examine the topic more fully through elaboration, clarification, comparison, contrast, justification, and evaluation.

Activity: Create Extended Discussion Cards, using the model below. Divide the class into groups of six. (Teachers may wish to use only a portion of the class for this activity. If so, individuals not involved in the discussion may observe their peers.) Distribute the Extended Discussion Cards to participants. If class size requires one group to have four or five members, give one or two students two cards; if there are fewer than four students, incorporate these students into other groups, making some of the groups consist of seven students. Give each extra student one card from an extra set. To insure a wide variety of responses, students should discuss a controversial topic of interest to them. Students should incorporate at random the statements/questions from the cards into the discussion at appropriate times. Though the language style may differ from that of the students, they should be encouraged to use the

51

Extended Discussion Cards

ELABORATION

"Could you go into that a little further?"

"I would expand on that idea by saying. . . ."

"I'm not sure how that applies. Could you build on that idea more?"

CLARIFICATION

"What exactly do you mean?"

"Do I understand you to mean . . . ?"

"Please provide an example to help me understand your point of view."

COMPARISON

"That is an interesting statement. How does that compare with what was previously said?"

"I would compare that to. . . ."

"I see the following similarities in the ideas presented so far. . . ."

CONTRAST

"How would you contrast your idea to the one that (name of student) gave previously?"

"In contrast to your statement, I think. . . ."

"I see that idea as different from his/hers in this way. . . ."

JUSTIFICATION

"How would you defend that statement against . . . ?"

"What assumptions are you basing that on?"

"I think that idea/solution would work because. . . ."

EVALUATION

"My reaction to that idea is. . . ."

"What do you think of that idea?"

"I think my idea/solution is better because. . . ."

statement/question as it appears on the card so that observers may note when a specific type of statement is used. For example, in a discussion of the parable of the good Samaritan, Mary says, "It is more logical for the priest and Levite to have stopped." Bob, wanting Mary to justify her position, says, "What assumptions are you basing that on?" (Justification Card #2) Mary, in responding, is extending the discussion beyond the surface level.

TOPICS FOR DISCUSSION

Listed below are topics which may be used with the following activities: Contributions, Summary-Agreement-Opinion, Interaction Cards. Role-Playing Cards, Extended Discussion Cards.

1. Church and state should not be separated.
2. The Bible should be taken literally.
3. Women's Liberation contradicts the role of women as presented in the Bible.
4. The church's first obligation is to the need of the community (local, state, national, and international) rather than to itself.
5. A person's life-style should not prohibit him/her from church membership.
6. Sustaining life by artificial means is against God's will.
7. The ecumenical movement will strengthen the Christian community.

BIBLIOGRAPHY

Bormann, Ernest, and Bormann, Nancy, *Effective Small Group Communication.* Minneapolis: Burgess Publishing Company, 1972.

Borton, Terry, *Reach, Touch and Teach.* New York: McGraw-Hill Book Company, 1970.

Boy, Angelo, and Pine, Gerald, *Expanding the Self: Personal Growth for Teachers.* Dubuque, Iowa: William C. Brown Company, Publishers, 1971.

Brooks, William D., *Speech Communication.* Dubuque, Iowa: William C. Brown Company, Publishers, 1971.

Brown, Charles T., and Keller, Paul W., *Monologue to Dialogue: An Exploration of Interpersonal Communication.* Englewood Cliffs, N.J.: Prentice-Hall, Inc., 1973.

Brown, George I., *Human Teaching for Human Learning: An Introduction to Confluent Education.* New York: The Viking Press, 1971.

Campbell, James H., and Hepler, Hal W., *Dimensions in Communication—Readings.* Belmont, Calif.: Wadsworth Publishing Company, Inc., 1966.

Clark, Tony, and Bock, Doug, *Is That You Out There?* Columbus, Ohio: Charles E. Merrill Publishing Company, 1973.

Coleman, Lyman, *Serendipity Frog-Kissin' Workshops.* Waco, Tex.: Serendipity House, 1974.

——————, *Breaking Free.* Waco, Tex.: Serendipity House, 1972.

——————, *Celebration.* Waco, Tex.: Serendipity House, 1972.

——————, *Discovery.* Waco, Tex.: Serendipity House, 1972.

——————, *Serendipity.* Waco, Tex.: Serendipity House, 1972.

Crowell, Laura, *Discussion: Method of Democracy.* Glenview, Ill.: Scott, Foresman and Company, 1963.

Flynn, Elizabeth W., and LaFaso, John F., *Designs in Affective Education: A Teacher Resource Program for Junior and Senior High.* New York: Paulist Press, 1974.

Fox, Robert; Luszk, Margaret B.; and Schmuck, Richard, *Problem Solving in the Classroom,* Chicago: Science Research Associates, Inc., 1970.

Giffen, Kim, and Patton, Bobby, eds., *Basic Readings in Interpersonal Communication.* New York: Harper & Row, Publishers, 1971.

Giffen, Kim, and Patton, Bobby, *Fundamentals of Interpersonal Communication.* New York: Harper & Row, Publishers, 1971.

Goffman, E., *The Presentation of Self in Everyday Life.* New York: Anchor Books, imprint of Doubleday & Company, Inc., 1959.

Gorman, Alfred H., *Teachers and Learners: The Interactive Process of Education.* Boston: Allyn & Bacon, Inc., 1974.

Gulley, Halbert E., *Discussion, Conference, and Group Process.* New York: Holt, Rinehart and Winston, 1960.

Hall, Edward T., *The Hidden Dimension.* New York: Doubleday & Company, Inc., 1966.

_____, *The Silent Language.* New York: Doubleday & Company, Inc., 1959.

Hamachek, Don, *Encounters with Self.* New York: Holt, Rinehart and Winston, 1971.

Hare, A. P., et al., *Small Groups: Studies in Social Interaction.* New York: Alfred A. Knopf, Inc., 1955.

Harris, Thomas A., *I'm OK—You're OK.* New York: Harper & Row, Publishers, 1969.

Howe, Leland W., and Howe, Mary, *Personalizing Education: Values Clarification and Beyond.* New York: Hart Publishing Co., Inc., 1975.

Johnson, David W., *Reaching Out: Interpersonal Effectiveness and Self Actualization.* Englewood Cliffs, N. J.: Prentice-Hall, Inc., 1972.

Jones, Richard M., *Fantasy and Feeling in Education.* New York: New York University Press, 1968.

Krupar, Karen, *The Application of Game Theory to Communication Training.* New York: The Free Press, division of Macmillan, Inc., 1973.

_____, *Communication Games.* New York: The Free Press, division of Macmillan, Inc., 1973.

Lewis, Howard, and Streitfield, Harold, *Growth Games.* New York: Harcourt Brace Jovanovich, Inc., 1971.

Luft, Joseph, *Group Processes: An Introduction to Group Dynamics,* rev. ed. Palo Alto, Calif.: National Press Books, 1970.

Lyon, Harold C., *Learning to Feel: Feeling to Learn.* Columbus, Ohio: Charles E. Merrill Publishing Company, 1971.

Maslow, Abraham, *Toward a Psychology of Being.* New York: D. Van Nostrand Company, 1962.

McCroskey, James C.; Larson, Carl E.; and Knapp, Mark L., *An Introduction to Interpersonal Communication.* Englewood Cliffs, N. J.: Prentice-Hall, Inc., 1971.

Mortensen, O. D., *Communication: The Study of Human Interaction*. New York: McGraw-Hill Book Company, 1972.

Nierenberg, Gerard, and Calero, Henry, *How to Read a Person Like a Book*. New York: Pocket Books, division of Simon & Schuster, Inc., 1973.

Nyberg, David, *Tough and Tender Learning*. Palo Alto, Calif.: National Press Books, 1970.

Otto, Herbert A., *Group Methods Designed to Actualize Human Potential*. Beverly Hills, Calif.: The Holistic Press, 1968.

Powell, John, *Why Am I Afraid to Love?* rev. ed. Niles, Ill.: Argus Communications, 1967.

Rein, Irving J., *Rudy's Red Wagon: Communication Strategies in Contemporary Society*. Glenview, Ill.: Scott, Foresman and Company, 1972.

Rogers, Carl, *Freedom to Learn*. Columbus, Ohio: Charles E. Merrill Publishing Company, 1969.

Rosenfeld, Lawrence B., *Human Interaction in the Small Group Setting*. Columbus, Ohio: Charles E. Merrill Publishing Company, 1973.

Schrank, Jeffrey, *Media in Value Education: A Critical Guide*. Niles, Ill.: Argus Communications, 1970.

Schutz, William, *Joy*. New York: Ballantine Books, Inc., 1973.

Shaw, M. E., *Group Dynamics*. New York: McGraw-Hill Book Company, 1971.

Shostrom, Everett, *Man, the Manipulator*. Nashville: Abingdon Press, 1967.

Simon, Sidney; Howe, Leland; and Kirschenbaum, Howard, *Values Clarification*. New York: Hart Publishing Co., Inc., 1972.

Stanford, Gene, and Stanford, Barbara Dodds, *Learning Discussion Skills Through Games*. Delmar, N.Y.: Citation Press, imprint of Scholastic Book Services, 1969.

Stanford, Gene, "Taming Restless Cats: Alternatives to the Whip." *English Journal,* vol. 62 (November, 1973), pp. 1127-1132.

Stanford, Gene, and Roark, Albert E., *Human Interaction in Education.* Boston: Allyn & Bacon, Inc., 1974.

Stewart, John, ed., *Bridges Not Walls: A Book About Interpersonal Communication.* Reading, Mass.: Addison-Wesley Publishing Co., Inc., 1973.

Torrance, E. Paul, *Encouraging Creativity in the Classroom.* Dubuque, Iowa: William C. Brown Company, Publishers, 1970.